YOUNG RAIN

Kevin Hart was born in 1954 in the village of Ockenden near London, and grew up in London and Brisbane. He has published several books of poetry in Britain, Australia and America, including *Flame Tree: Selected Poems* (Bloodaxe Books, 2002) and his latest collection, *Young Rain* (Bloodaxe Books, 2009). His award-winning poetry has been translated into several languages, including Chinese. He is also the author of several volumes of literary criticism and theology. He teaches in the Department of Religious Studies at the University of Virginia in Charlottesville.

Kevin Hart
YOUNG RAIN

"Urbane & sophisticated
yet wholly
inclusive"

p 49

BLOODAXE BOOKS

Copyright © Kevin Hart 2009

ISBN: 978 1 85224 829 1

First published in the UK in 2009 by
Bloodaxe Books Ltd,
Highgreen,
Tarset,
Northumberland NE48 1RP
and by Notre Dame University Press in the USA
and Giramondo in Australia

www.bloodaxebooks.com
For further information about Bloodaxe titles
please visit our website or write to
the above address for a catalogue.

Bloodaxe Books Ltd acknowledges
the financial assistance of
Arts Council England, North East.

LEGAL NOTICE

All rights reserved. No part of this book may be
reproduced, stored in a retrieval system, or
transmitted in any form, or by any means, electronic,
mechanical, photocopying, recording or otherwise,
without prior written permission from Bloodaxe Books Ltd.

Requests to publish work from this book
must be sent to Bloodaxe Books Ltd.

Kevin Hart has asserted his right under
Section 77 of the Copyright, Designs and Patents Act 1988
to be identified as the author of this work.

This project has been assisted by the Australian Government through
the Australia Council for the Arts, its arts funding and advisory body.

Cover design: Neil Astley & Pamela Robertson-Pearce.

Printed in Great Britain by Bell & Bain Limited, Glasgow, Scotland.

For Rita

ACKNOWLEDGEMENTS

Acknowledgements are due to the editors of the following publications in which some of these poems first appeared: *Agenda, The Antioch Review, Antipodes, Arena, Eureka Street, The Gettysburg Review, The Harvard Review, The Literary Review, The London Review, Manoa, Meanjin, Poetry Daily, The Prague Review, Prism, Salt, Salt-Lick Quarterly, slope, Southerly, Space, Stonewall* and *Verse*.

Several poems appeared in *Poésie Australienne*, edited by Chris Wallace-Crabbe and Simone Kadi (UVHC Press, Valenciennes, 2002), and 'Nights' ('There's nothing that I really want...') appeared in the *Alhambra Poetry Calendar 2009* (Belgium). 'Night Music' was published, along with artwork by Kristin Headlam, as an artist's book of the same title in 2003 by Lexicon House, Melbourne, while others appeared in a chapbook, *Dark Retreat* (Vagabond Press, Sydney, 2005). 'Birthday Card' appeared in *The Fifth Question and After: Poems for Tomaž Šalamun* published by Vagabond Press in 2001, and two parts of 'Night Music' appeared in *The Indigo Book of Modern Australian Sonnets* (2003), edited by Geoff Page. Several poems were first published in *Best Australian Poems, 2003*, edited by Peter Craven (Black Inc Press) and *Best Australian Poems, 2006*, edited by Judith Beveridge (University of Queensland Press); others were broadcast by the Australian Broadcasting Commission in 'Poetica' and by Radio Antwerp.

Several poems are reprinted with permission from the final section of *Flame Tree: Selected Poems* (Bloodaxe Books, UK, 2002; Paper Bark Press, 2003).

Some lines from 'The Clock' are taken from a case study analysed by Franz Fischer, 'Raum-Zeit-Struktur und Denkstörung in der Schizophrenie,' *Zeitschrift für die gesamte Neurologie und Psychiatrie* 124 (1930), 247-49. I wish to thank Gloria Davies for her help in rendering Chinese poems into English, and Henry Weinfield for loaning me his acute eyes and ears.

CONTENTS

1

- 11 My Name
- 12 That Life
- 13 Finland
- 14 Snow
- 15 Yes
- 16 The Word
- 17 Inside
- 18 Bread
- 19 Round
- 20 Summer
- 21 Summer Rain
- 22 Nights
- 23 A Sleeping Girl
- 24 Prayer

2

- 26 Amo te Solo

3

- 38 Night
- 39 Here
- 40 The Great Truths
- 41 To Think of You Tonight
- 42 At the Barbizon
- 43 The Past
- 44 The Clock
- 45 Hands
- 46 T'ang Retreat
- 46   1 *The Trader's Wife*
- 47   2 *How My Roof Blew Away*
- 48 Thinking of David Campbell
- 49 Birthday Card
- 50 Nights
- 51 Reading St Gregory of Nyssa
- 52 Lightning Words
- 54 'We talked of prayer, that night'
- 55 Prayer

	4
59	Night Music

	5
70	Dark Retreat
80	Mud

1

My Name

There is a silence words can't touch.
And there's a name inside my name
Though one my mother never said out loud

She never said it, never once, although
She knew there was another name
That sleeps inside my name

Sleep now, old name,
For no one wants to know of you

My mother, she is dead these dozen years
And she is grown so small
She sleeps inside my name when it is said

I think she sleeps
Within that other name as well, more deeply, far
More quietly, turning only once or twice
Inside that paradise

Sleep now, old love,
It is too late to say a word to you

That Life

There is a life I've barely lived at all
And, summer afternoons, I feel it brush
Against me, heading somewhere far away,

Up in the north perhaps where rain comes down
As if just thrown in vengeance for some wrong
No one remembers now, though people talk,

And in that life I stroll through open doors
And take the darkness offered every night
And am bewildered still by clocks and eyes.

It touches me, that breath, say once a year,
When rain hits thick and hard against the door,
When I have let my darkness have its way,

And then I almost know that other world,
And live in small hard words from years ago
And cannot be at peace in any life.

Finland

I could stay here all day inside my house
Or go to Finland.

'There is a hotel in the north,'
A friend told me, 'that's made of ice.'
'You're never cold at night
'Because they heap thick reindeer skins all over you.'

I warm to the idea
But part of me likes it right here
Where I have always lived, not looking out too far.
And so the years go by

And my life changes, once just every year or so,
Now almost month by month –
Like when you're on that new fast train

That glides up north
And Finland becomes Lapland between lunch and tea.

There are new vowels to hear,
Long lists of things that you must do without

And that is why I want to go

And why I will not go:
I know those lean old towns where no one walks

And I can do without
Those streets made endless by the sun or lack of sun.

I have those lists at home:

And I can do without.

Snow

Some days
The snow has taken me in
To know the time of snow, to live
Inside a world so quiet

Its music
Is all a shimmering. Some evenings
When quite alone
I turn off every light

And watch the snow
Enjoy the dark, moving lushly
Through spiky air,
Finding more time

In time
Than when I stretch myself
And am
My father's father. Oh yes,

There is
A sparkling choir, there surely is,
And dark ice air
Through which we fall

Yes

It happens, once or twice. Oh yes,
It happens
On days that go astray, warm days
When light is rich and hours are long.
It happens

When time
Is inside-out a little, when you see
Those flakes of cloud
Float up, as if released from the snowy lawn,
And those red cedar leaves are still:

Oh yes, it happens,
Although they cannot say exactly so
Although we cannot tell them how
Although – it happens,
Just once or twice, but yes, oh yes.

The Word

Say *wood* and everything is clean again.
The word is all around you, like the night,
Impossible to grasp. Your mouth is dark.

A splinter found its way into your quick.
That old tree slit by lightning won't be moved.
Last year's thin rain froze hard inside a trunk

And now a honey flesh shines through cracked bark.
Your mouth is dark. Go far into yourself,
Let quietness gather there, then say the word.

Inside

Some fourteen years ago
My mother surely died
(One of her dresses breathes
Beside my father's suit)

My father lives alone
Inside a small dark house;
He walks from room to room
Inside his afterlife

One day that suit will come
Folded beside a dress
(I walk from room to room
Inside my mother's death)

Bread

How strange it is that there are loaves of bread.
They come out hot from deep inside our fear
And there's a light that lasts for several days
(In spring it dances through the evening.)

You never cut a loaf that's just been baked.
You let it sit and teach you many things
Your mother never told you when alive.
How good it is that there are loaves of bread.

Round

The river says, 'I am so poor,'
My father whispers, 'I must die,'
And the warm stone sleeps long and hard
And yes the hand will need the eye.

Brightly the river prays, 'O sea!'
Darkly my father's words disband,
And the warm stone sleeps long and hard
And yes the eye recalls the hand.

The river says, 'I am so rich,'
My father breathes his death all day,
And the warm stone sleeps long and hard
And yes the eye will turn away.

Summer

A trip to the corner shop will take all day
But what the fuck: you need a can of Coke.
You see the air is wrinkled like your shirt
        And feel at home

With those young blokes all lounging round with beer
And a TV just chirping with the cricket,
Then there's the guy who teaches something French
        Hosing his car,

And the youngish wife outside with her long legs
And her big husband off in Singapore
For what must be his second month up there
        Doing software:

There's more to say, you know, about the booze,
The crying in the backyard late at night,
About the smell of thunder in the dark
        And that walk back.

Summer Rain

Fine tapered glasses filled with 'Passing Clouds'
And everywhere the smell of summer rain;

I had got home an hour before, and cooked
A flounder slightly stunned by mango sauce.

We sat outside, in cane armchairs, and talked
About some Dante you had read in class,

Some words all blossom, others deep old wine.
Late summer: it was in the air that night,

And when I came to fill your glass again
I found that we were kissing long and slow

Although we hardly knew each other well,
Although your Dante told us it was wrong:

Sweet words and silences I almost knew
About, well, talking, flying, making love.

It didn't matter all that much, that night.

Nights

There's nothing that I really want:
The stars tonight are rich and cold
Above my house that vaguely broods
Upon a path soon lost in dark.

My dinner plate is chipped all round
(It tells me that I've changed a lot)
My glass is cracked all down one side
(It shows there is a path for me).

My hands – I rest my head on them.
My eyes – I rest my mind on them.
There's nothing that I really need
Before I set out on that path.

A Sleeping Girl

Today you climbed our neighbor's tallest tree:
'I got so high you couldn't touch my foot.'

It's true: all afternoon I've felt that gap,
And now I climb the stairs to read to you

I find you're tightly tucked into yourself.
Your mother says that when we fall asleep

Over a tale, our faces are the same.
I know that I can count on times like that

For two years, tops. No need to look outside:
I know full well the tree that I have climbed.

Prayer

O come, in any way you want,
In morning sunlight fooling in the leaves
Or in thick bouts of rain that soak my head

> *Because of what the darkness said*

Or come, though far too slowly for my eye to see,
Like a dark hair that fades to gray

Come with the wind that wraps my house

Or winter light that slants upon a page

> *Because the beast is stirring in its cage*

Or come in raw and ragged smells
Of gum leaves dangling down at noon
Or in the undertow of love
When she's away

> *Because a night creeps through the day*

Come as you used to, years ago,
When I first fell for you

In the deep calm of an autumn morning
Beginning with the cooing of a dove

> *Because of love, the lightest love*

Or if that's not your way these days
Because of me, because
Of something dead in me,
Come like a jagged knife into my gut

> *Because your touch will surely cut*

Come any way you want

But come

2

Amo te Solo

Sometimes a life goes wrong
Without an evil deed:
So here I am in Berne
Awake in the white hours
Waiting for time to pass
Until I can call home

>   *For when I am away*
>   *Each hour leaves its bruise*

Late home, my cab drives down
Small streets whose names I love;
The evening is ripe
With sparrows and a breeze;
An outside light shines round
And tightly holds the house

>   *There is no life on earth*
>   *I would not spend with you*

Love is a standing to attention. Yes,
No man can argue long against a truth
That smashes hard into his deepest life

It's Spring: the maple tree speaks of her lips,
The curve around her bottom that I love.
But no one sane will ever quote a tree

So I must tell her how this little world
Is bigger now only because of her,
And how this massive universe makes sense

Only because of her (it does, it does),
And how this ordinary room is love
And truth because she walks through it all day

There are three days before I'm home with you
And I hate every one. It's summertime:
The afternoon was swollen, evening
      Is guava pulp,

And lovers loll around on Lygon Street.
Ah, let them all make love deliciously
And let the days go bush because of them
      All sleeping in.

There are three days inside me, waiting there,
And each one whispers of your long smooth legs,
The feel of them under a cotton sheet
      Then round my head.

You whispered in my ear. You wanted me
To touch you somewhere new,

And while one hand was roaming round my thigh
Your other one took mine

And led it like a child around your waist
To where your dress was loose,

And then you held me hard with both your arms
And said I was the one.

(You said I was a one
That day you held me hard with both your arms:

It made your dress go loose –
'Like when I was a girl' – around your waist;

Your hand was taking mine,
The other one was roaming round my thigh,

'To touch you somewhere new,'
You whispered in my ear. You wanted me.)

Let's go to bed all afternoon
(But pull that blind down to the sill,
The sunlight must not see us here)

I don't mind giving day the flick
(My fingers can unbutton jeans,
My tongue knows yours and where it goes)

This darkness gives me all your voice
(Your cries are carved into my back,
My hands will wander where they will)

But there are little hairs I love
(I feel them high upon your thighs,
They make my fingertips go faint)

And there's a mole I want to kiss
(It's on your shoulder, that I know,
But which one is a mystery)

So raise that blind an inch or two
(The breeze will push in when it can,
The blind will bang against the pane)

Today,
For no good reason, I thought
How your left thigh
Is curved to my right hand, and how
My palm slides up a little way
When you pull back
And push your bottom out;

And thought
How much you like all that, and
How much you like
Me pulling your red shirt over
Your sweet shoulder, kissing you there,
How fine you are
So wild under my belt

As though
You wanted, oh so hard, to
Touch my shirttail
And find out where it's been of late;
And thought, until my mind was numb,
How long it is
Until you get back home

There is an hour that holds no time at all
And then I wake, and haven't been asleep,

And so come back, as though a lifetime late,
To this strange thing, my body, which you love,

And find it quick with blood and sight, and raised
To the power of two, because I sense you, here,

In this big house, with its routines and life,
Upstairs, maybe, just flapping out fresh sheets

On a bed we know and surely trust by now
That will not speak a word of what we do

If a siren kicks and screams and flails its arms
When we are making love,
My finger slowly moving up your thigh
Will not put out the fire
I've worked all evening to burn in you,

And if you start to kiss
The whole admiring, eager length of me
And only get half way
When a tornado starts its crazy swirl
Just let the house blow down,

And if fierce February rain breaks through
The blinds into our room
While you are reaching down, way down, my pants
The chairs can float away
And our old bed can thump against the wall

Just sometimes when we talk there is a word
I like to hear, often on summer days

When kissing you and lifting up your skirt:
It holds a silence deep inside, that word,

And when you whisper it into my ear
That silence quickly blossoms into calm,

And my right hand works o so quietly there
Although, it must be said, you are not calm

When kissing me, your small hands moving fast,
My shirttail hanging over my loose belt,

And that rich word now entering my ear
All finely covered with your young hot breath

Fuck off, fat clock – I want her now,
Not some fine day you might allow.
It is her voice I long to hear,
It is her mouth I want, her rear
All smiling on my lap (and how!)

You're clogged with time, a sad white cow
That's not been milked. Ah, let it flow,
Old thing. You won't? Well then, my dear,
      Fuck off, fat clock.

Don't like my tone? Don't want a row?
Don't want my big fist going *POW!?*
Then let a week slip by round here
(And nowhere else – you're in the clear).
But if you won't give time the throw,
      Fuck off, fat clock.

It is a dark green ivy afternoon
In Princes' Hill as rain falls through vast trees
Into the little garden where we live
    On summer days.

It's late December and the clocks have stopped
While people watch their windows come alive
And old tin roofs out back get hopping mad
    And gutters booze.

Last week we burned our flesh, but now we baste
While smoky jazz just cruises down the lane
And makes out with our cat beneath a car
    While we're in bed,

The sheets all trampled underneath our feet,
Those lyrics touching us as night comes on:
Something about a day spent drinking wine
    And getting laid

3

Night

I walk outside and look straight at the stars.
Today a letter scraped my skin away.

I cannot bear the light, I simply can't.
Now even these dead things are hurting me.

Here

In a bare room where light pours in from the ocean
You are still sleeping
You are still here

And nothing more happens except the sound
Of a page turning
While you sleep on

The sound of a story turning and the ocean stirring
Near our thin room
With you asleep

Perhaps with the thought of a storm much later on
When you awake
In this bruised room

Two people still here perhaps with ocean light
Fragile and turning
Dark as your voice

That lives in the air and mirrors here. But look,
You are awake;
I am still here.

The Great Truths

So we run out of world, not time:
Life hangs around like last night's gin,
And even if we peel away
The morning light from dappled things

There is no chance that we will see
This fountain pen left on a chair
For what it is. The world is love
No matter what we make of it,

No matter how we cut it up:
The pen must know a hand on it.
The great truths live just out of sight,
Past what I know of you, or you

Of me: so let's be calm and kind
Until the great truths come to us
In that gold light we've heard about
And pens fly quickly to our hands

To Think of You Tonight
(after Pedro Salinas)

To think of you tonight
Was not to think of you, not me alone
With just my thoughts. The whole wide world was there
Along with me, and thinking you all through the night.

The long deep sleep of meadows, stars,
The silent sea, and grass
Known only from its bitter scent,
Ah, everything –
Red giants, cicadas, ants – was thinking you.

Small stones
Reached out toward the stars,
Embracing quiet water, trembling trees
And me
Who offered all of it to you. And everything
Said yes to you!
The light and shade went hand in hand
To a higher light of loving you, the endless silence
Of earth and those soft voices of the clouds,
They joined
In the Song of Songs I had become.
The world and everyone in it
Agreed, desire and time made peace
Inside me, dear, as when your kiss is mine as well.
And then
I nearly stopped loving you to love you more,
To give the joy of loving you to the vast night
That roams through time, ambassador
Of love turned into stars and quietness and world,
All saved from fear
Of those we lay out here when we forget.

At the Barbizon

Late afternoon, just lying on the bed,
And then a sorrow rises in the room.
I look outside: it's not Manhattan, no,
And not my suitcase with its old new clothes.

A sorrow fills the room; the walls are close.
It's not the telephone that doesn't sing,
It's not the wine and empty glasses there,
It's not the mirror staring blankly back.

The walls are close; New York looks quickly in
And finds a long hair clinging to my shirt.
It's you, my love, you've come this far with me!
And so I lay it quietly on my face.

I should be getting in my suit by now,
I should be thinking of important men,
But even though I hear the clock go mad
I cannot move beneath that single hair.

The Past

I used to see her in a sandwich shop
On Brunswick Road. She made me toasted cheese.
I liked her ponytail and gypsy scarf,

I liked her running shoes and sawn off jeans,
I liked a little bruise beneath her knee,
And so my sandwiches got high with ham:

They dripped with mayonnaise and frayed with sprouts
While I just gazed at her and murmured, 'Swiss;
Tomatoes; onion; lettuce; pepper; salt.'

I had to ask her out: my sandwiches
Had got too big to eat! We lived off Smith,
I did Philosophy, and wrote all day –

'Is Death Impossible?' – and jumped on her
The moment she was home from work at five.
Our neighbour was a physicist, and yarned

Of flavoured quarks and tachions, those things
That speed into the past, and wrote SF
About a 'tachion machine': a burst

Would put you with the apes or dinosaurs
While very few would nudge you back a week.
'What would you like on that?' Susanna asked

When kissing me in bed. 'The lot,' I'd say.
Some nights I'd wake up scared to hell by time.
Susanna was still there, in white whipped sheets,

And sleepily I'd hold her tight, and hold
Our evening tight, and whisper to the dark,
'Release a tachion – just one, just one.'

The Clock

What should I do with the clock?
I always have to look at it,
For there is so much time

When you're away from clocks and all
When you're not here with me –
In Chile, Mexico or Spain,

In one of those brown words
That taste as if they're flush with oil;
It tears itself apart

That clock up there, up on the wall,
What should I do with it?
I always have to look at it

For there is so much time;
I think you come and stretch it hard
Until it sags like gum

And long whole weeks go by like cows
Across the dusty plain;
It's getting lost in me, that clock,

I feel its hands inside
And you're not here in me with words
And there is so much time

Hands

O you must learn,
My mother said, o you must learn
To tell, she said,
To tell – and paused, just waving hands –
To tell the time,

And gave a cardboard clock
With hands,
With hands that I could move
To make it as I wished
And so I learned

That I could make, o make it just
Just as I told it,
And not unmake it, as I told
And told it time and time again.
No use for it,

I learned and did not learn:
My mother lived and waved her hands
And did not live
And waved her hands
And then her hands were still

T'ang Retreat

1 *The Trader's Wife*
(after Li Bo)

When hair was hardly covering my brow
I was out plucking blossom in the sun.
You rode up smartly on your bamboo horse
And chased me round the garden, throwing plums:

Two kids, without a second thought to share,
Both growing up in a small river town.
At fourteen, now your wife, I was so shy
I lived in corners, head forever bowed,

And never once, not once, came round to you.
By fifteen I had learned to smile with you,
And longed to be with you, like ash and dust
Impossible to part! When you were far

You were still here, as steady as my heart,
And so I never thought to scan the road.
At sixteen, trading took you way out west,
Out past those boiling rapids with that rock

Where gibbons thump their chests and screech all night.
Here, by our gate, you held my hand an hour,
The moss grew green and thick in your slow steps:
I sweep the fallen leaves, but it sticks hard.

The autumn winds came quick and cold this year;
September's here, and yellow butterflies
Flit by the garden bed, always in pairs.
I cannot look at them: a lonely face

Will sometimes find a way into my own.
One day you will return, and when you know
Please write and say. I'll leave at once, upstream,
And come as close as sailors think it safe.

2 How My Roof Blew Away
(after Du Fu)

November, and the winds of autumn shriek
And roll the thatch, three deep, right off our roof
Into the river and the paddy field:

Some catches in high branches of the peach,
Some plops into a swirling, muddy pool.
A gang of kids blows in from out of town,

They know I'm old, and look me in the eye
And make right off with thatch through thick bamboo.
I scream at them until I've lost my voice,

Limp back, lean on a cane, and shake with rage.
The wind calms down, but all the clouds bleed ink
No matter where I look! Our threadbare quilt

Is only cotton, thin as frost, and ripped;
My children toss at night, stick feet right through.
The roof is rich with drips; there's no escape –

And rain pours thickly down, like strings of hemp.
I hardly sleep these days at best of times,
And now I'm face to face with dark all night.

If I could have a mansion, full of rooms,
The poor could come and shelter from the cold,
A mansion made of stone that won't blow down,

If only I could glimpse that great warm house
Filled like a honeycomb with peace and calm,
I'd freeze to death right here without complaint.

Thinking of David Campbell

Long in the shower, then a knock
    And then a friend told me
That you had died. What could I do?

Water was dripping down
    My face, and someone had turned off
    A light on half my world

And now that I am twice as old
    I still can't find the switch
Although I stop to talk with you

    Say once a month or more
And smell you as you pass through me
    Say once a year or so

And know then nothing much has changed,
    That you look out for me
For no good reason, since our days

    Were very few to count
But overfull for me. Dear friend,
    There's nothing new to say

Since nothing happened since you left
    Except I put on years
And can it be – I think it must –

    That since I write to you
Once in ten years you may expect
    Two poems more, then me.

Birthday Card

A sad young man stood quietly in the sky.
'Don't jump,' I yelled, 'you'll never get to read
'The poetry of Tomaž Šalamun...!'

He nearly died. But then he blinked, and slid
Straight down a fire escape and hugged me hard.
'You're right,' he said, 'I'll find another girl,'

Then walked me up to Lygon Street, and ate
The largest *osso buco* on the block.
A waiter brought us earthy southern wine,

The sort you get so cheap in Ljubljana
If you know where to go. I never did,
I'd stay inside my little box of tricks:

Was I a shepherd or a hunter? Why
Did melancholy pose those stumpers then?
And what the hell is that weird thingamie

That hovers over 'Tomaž Šalamun'?
I wanna get myself a piece of that,
Oh yes, I wanna be – wait – 'Keviš Harž'

Or maybe 'Čeviž Harš'...
                              Some days I rise
A little early, sit upon my roof
And look northwest, but have to use my stilts

To see the lights of Ljubljana shine.
Tomaž is there, I know, he's writing lines
That I will love. He must be sixty soon,

And when he is I'm sure he'll leap and wave:
I'll open up the softest red in town
And jump to him, and hand my friend a glass.

Nights

At times my name gets tired of me
And wanders off into the dark:
Some times it claws me with a bark
Some times it leaves me almost free

And then I cannot see a thing
And flesh is barely tied to soul:
Those nights the density of coal
Those nights when I am not a king

Then hours bunch up to watch me fall
And I am turned into a prayer:
Some nights I circle God's dark lair
Some nights an endless night is all

Reading St Gregory of Nyssa

A light snow takes over the afternoon
And sets me free: I pick up that old book

And start to read again. My Greek's gone bad
So snowflakes fall between the sentences

And make me see that it's like this, at first,
On life's far side: no words, souls in suspense

In grey-blue light that does not let you breathe,
A time that's void of time, except for snow

That floats, each flake made fresh with timeless care.
Perhaps in time we all will come to bliss,

Perhaps we will be turned around, and touch
The face of God, as do the stones and trees

Even in hours peeled back to bone. Ah now
The day is going bad, the wind's picked up

And hits the snowflakes horizontal, hard;
It smacks them on the oaks that just stand there

Until it's worse, then they reach out for help
But, driven wild, they lash out, strike and sway.

How many souls hunch there in that black wind
That screeches like torn steel! How many souls

Cling there, Dark One, cling there and pray that death
Not be like this for anyone they love.

Lightning Words

Old almond moonlight
This summer evening:

Burnt almonds
For the tongue

Thin moonlight
For the hungry pupil

A summer
For those who want rich days

And a long, deep evening
For the soul

*

Prayer,
That terrible, strange thing –

A soul
Unclenching something fierce to play

Hide-and-go-seek,
Or taking the first step, again,

Into a boat without oars
With evening falling fast,

Or leaping
From a cliff, no one around,

And hoping to be gripped
Halfway down

*

Father of the tall bruised days of summer
And lightning words

Of the child's first step
And smack just entering her vein

Of moonlight
Over the half-stoned girl raped in the park,

His hands clamped on her wrists,
His face a fist –

Ah, the game is over, Father, so come on out
And sit awhile

And tell her something soft and slow.
I have some faith in you,

And need far more. See, there it is,
A speck that glitters in the lamp's thin light –

'We talked of prayer, that night,'

You wrote, in your last words to me,
'And now – all *this*,' meaning
Each word had turned
Its back on you,
On me, on everyone you loved,

That 'night'
Had freed itself from talk and wine, had gone
Astray in other days
And scrawled itself in every word,
That 'we'

Was to be drained
Of new life, meaning 'life', leaving me
With your last words adjusting all your words,
Each one becoming dark,
That 'prayer'

Was left for me from you, for me and you,
Was brimming high
With all that darkness we had talked about,
That night and every night,
Even when talking of something else

Prayer

Break open my words,
Break them,
But only the words I speak to you alone

Those words at night

Old words

O let anything there is of prayer
Find you

       *

Crack them like cloves, Dark One,
Let all the silences between my words go up
With a perfume of *evening* and *wine*

With the caress of my wife's small hand
When she's asleep, O
When all my thoughts are fraying fast

But let the bitter words stay in my mouth
Let them stay here
With the dark blood of daylight words

       *

I offer up
Those nights I fall through dark for hour on hour
And wake o Lord
With *death* and *love* both preying on my mind

O rest your fingers there, between their claws,
And wrench me hard:

Don't let me set around myself,
Don't let me die as *me*

       *

I feel the darkness moving round me now
O Lord
Let it be you this time, o Lord, let it be you

4

Night Music

On summer nights up north rain falls asleep
And falls on Auchenflower: how sweet to slip

Down Lima Street and feel the river's pull
Toward Peru and want to stay at home

Because the starlight whispers in your eye
While roofs are running fast with fat loud rain,

Because the moon sweats light round Davies Park
And the great river broods upon its turn

Round Vulture Street and then beyond its ken,
And houses live halfway inside that care

And know by now no worry stops the wash
Of steaming mud over the cleanest hearth,

Yet watch that river concentrating hard
And young rain falling sharply on its back

Add music to the night and there is night,
Or, some nights, only music: deep inside,

Near breathing, a memory of blackberries
Down a cold lane I cannot place these days,

With no before or after: paper bag
Half full and wet, and – no, that's all there is,

A music by itself, these simple notes
Played with one finger on some icy keys

That slowly feel their way around the room:
The deeper ones say *blackberry* and *rain*

Though nothing more, no mother standing there,
No homing and no haunting: so add sound,

The chill of white keys, late, not music, no,
Night there, my hand a fist around the bag

A hand is moving there, in winter light,
My father's hand, or maybe grandfather's

Now that my father has become so old,
Now that his father isn't quite so fierce

Though he is dead these twenty years, but still
His hand must have its dreams inside the grave,

His hand will have its reasons there as well,
And maybe, winter afternoons, he thinks

We need to see his hand, a map of veins
And bones and gristle guiding me nowhere,

But maybe telling father how to find
A spoon that fell behind a plate last year,

Some fur upon his jumper from the cat,
That paper he put down a week ago

The day my mother died I was home late:
My lover told me bluntly at the door

And said that she was sorry but was best
To say it fast and get it over with.

It was. And mother would have done the same.
Then she prepared our tea. I heard her slice

Onions and carrots while I simply sat
And waited for the thought to cover me

So I could live inside it for a while.
The vegetables were hissing in a pan,

Evening was settling down on everything
And still the thought was very far away

(Or was it brooding there, in words not said,
Around a knife's old blade, inside the food?)

There is a darkness sleeping with the dark.
It knows no sun and never comes too close

But waits behind each little thing you see
And lets no shadow give its game away.

There are odd moments when you simply stop
For no good reason, then you see a clock

That seems to start again right then and there.
It wipes out what you never really knew.

There was a day you slowly kissed for hours,
There was a day you almost touched the night

And learned that you were neither one nor two
Because there is a darkness in the dark.

Hands moved around; a room grew old then young;
And in that night you heard another breathe

Some words will murmur only in the dark:
Not in the evening when folk come home

And talk about the day, how sunlight slid
Beneath that door or grazed a worker's cheek,

Not before midnight when the red slows down
Or fears are stretched out in another dream,

But when stray cats begin to smell the earth
And know dark rain will start to fall quite soon

And they must find a car that will not move,
Or when the silence seems a kind of food

For people walking late who cannot sleep
Because some words fall only in the dark:

Words without flesh, thin words, exhausted words,
Dark words that turn to silence on the tongue

Dear night, you know I am alone again
And so you play a little Schumann, quiet,

As it should always be, best heard, as now,
Across the street on a thick summer night.

My mother died, dear night, an hour like this,
The minutes moving very slowly, hot,

And trying to shake off what clothes there are.
No one was there to hold her hand, I think,

No one was there to say the simplest word:
Her last bed was a bed she never knew.

Dear night, I went there once, but very late,
And walked a corridor you knew full well

And thought of you and her together there,
Cicadas playing fiercely round neat beds

Some nights I walk the streets when I can't sleep
But what I want is never there to see:

I know the streetlights like to stretch my bones,
I know the universe is moving fast.

There's nowhere that I really want to go:
The truth is just as hard in my own house,

The grass puts down its roots right where I live.
And when at last I reach the river bend

I tell myself, as though I were a child,
God is the dark before the shadows came.

Some nights I chew a blade of summer grass,
Some nights I cut my hand when pulling it:

I tell myself, as though I were a child,
God is the dark before the shadows came

I'm thinking of a night I knew up north:
A thunderstorm had come and groaned and gone.

There was a girl I took down by the river:
We let mosquitoes have our arms for free,

We let each other's hands go where they would.
I'm thinking of a night I knew up north,

It was the largest night I ever knew
(A thunderstorm had come and groaned and gone)

And water dripped right down from leaves on high.
There was a girl I took down by the river,

A girl I loved, though she is long since gone.
We let mosquitoes have our arms for free,

We saw the river carry branches fast
(We let each other's hands go where they would)

In Brisbane death was always very big:
At evening it swept in from the bay

And fell across the streets in vast flat sheets.
Some nights when air was only thick wet heat

I thought it tightly coiled inside me too
And one fine day it would flap through my mouth.

But death gets smaller with each year I live,
Today it looks me fairly in the face.

In Brisbane now my father cannot sleep
Because it's summer and because he's old,

He walks around his house alone at night
And picks up cushions, letters, even stamps,

Because he's looking hard for something small,
Something not long ago he held by hand

5

Dark Retreat

Dark One, it is the summer now: the evenings feel
Beneath my shirt, and it is good.
The trees, they sway a little when they get high,
And higher still the nests and stars are quiet.

Those wasps my children fear
Are tight in their mud house, near lax electric wires,
And those two girls, dipped in a humid day,
Are deepening in sleep;

And I am left alone
With you inside those wild electric wires out there
And playing with my half-unbuttoned shirt
And growing in those shady leaves

And in a black and yellow summer sting

Hide me, Dark One,
The things of day are strong:
Horizons pass
An inch away from me
And I must rest

And wait for you
And wait for all the night
Turned in at last
Turned inside out all night;
I cannot sleep

And cannot cross
The shortest word to you –
Horizons stretch
And in their space I make
My dark retreat

With open eyes
That watch for all the night:
For all the night
The things of night are strong
Hide me, Dark One

There is a secret place
I've seldom been
These forty years;
And weeks and months
Grow thick
In forty years.

I went there yesterday
When someone left
A clock ajar:
There was no dust,
Only the faintest smell
Of half-drunk milk;

And you were there,
Dark One,
Not changed a bit:
I slept with you
And when I woke
The years were light

Some nights I smell my mother's neck,
>   Her fat, loose breath,
>   And know she isn't far away,
Though when I turn she surely won't be there.

Dark One, you know me to the bone,
>   You scrape my heart
>   And find too much that frightens me.
The dead are yours, I know; but still I turn.

A single word can darken the widest room
Even in summer:
                  glass all through my bread
For year on year

                  Yet I would give
This sunburned air for just one word,
Dark One,

Even a word that filled my mouth with blood;

But you keep quiet,
Just hiding there, behind my death,
For year on year

                  Your voice –
I would give up this champagne light

To know it just once more,
Even if sheathed in a sparrow's song,

A flash
Of a sparrow's outstretched wings,

Or the memory of that sparrow
That smashed into my windowpane
In a black storm

It's winter now, Dark One,
No light worth speaking of:
Fat flakes of snow;
My watch face down
Beside the bed

I let myself go still
And time spurts out
Of every pore;
Then, very slowly,
You enter me

Take me to a dark site,
O Lord, a false light sticks
To every part of me;

There are so few nearby,
So many grim with light –
Your dark is hard to find:

My father – he is dark
My wife – o she is dark
They are not far: take me

It's true, Dark One,
I gulp down time
With smiling girls
Or waste my days
With leaves that glow
With inner light

I want, oh yes,
To be so strong –
A row of teeth;
And maybe then
Bad men will speak
Of you with love

But I doubt it:
And, even now,
She touches me;
Oh yes, Dark One,
I want all this
With you one day

Untuned Spring: the young grass flirts
With stringy weeds; the tanagers
Sing with a splash of Spanish; wind
Saves gobs of old man snow in shade.

Between big awkward chords, I push
Stiff windows high, tack on new screens,
And taste this sweet old thing: chill air
That's brushed some baby leaves of oak.

You're here as well, Dark One, so where's
Your hidey hole? The kettle's hiss,
My daughter's drawing of our cat,
That crumbling wasp nest by the door?

Ah, close your eyes
And let him come:
Dark One
(It will not take so long
If you are still)

See, there is fruit
Asleep in a dish
And far beneath the house
The wine is deep
(Now close your eyes)

There is a loss
That weighs less
Than a smile, more than the sun
(And girls can pick it up
On entering a room):

Dark One
Can cancel that, oh yes
My wild one will
(And apples and oranges will shine
In your old bowl)

Mud

I think it is the smell of mangrove mud
Caught as you pass Whyte Island, just before
The old refinery gets into gear,
    That you love most,

The thick wild stench of that raw mud, oh yes
I think you wander there and drink it in
On days before those pipes and cylinders
    Were ever thought,

And spend long hours with every slow rich curve
As my fat river deepens some and sleeps;
You lay right down in it and float away
    Past squiggly creeks

(And yet, at night, I think you want to be
Where water threads those seventeen small rocks:
We met there, Dark One, all those years ago.
    You smelled of mud).